by Polly Peterson
illustrated by Baurrox

Harcourt

Orlando   Boston   Dallas   Chicago   San Diego

Visit *The Learning Site!*
www.harcourtschool.com

All day long, people travel from
one place to another. Everywhere
you look, there are people on the go!

Children are going to school.
Mothers and fathers are going to
work. People are going on short
trips and long journeys. There are
so many ways to travel!

People travel on foot. They walk to school and to work. They walk to stores and to the doctor's office. Walking is a good way to get from here to there.

Sometimes people walk just for fun. They go on hikes in the woods. They stroll through a park with a friend.

People travel on bicycles. Bicycles can take people around the block or across town. Riding a bicycle is faster than walking.

Sometimes people ride bicycles just for fun. Others ride on scooters or skateboards. It feels good to get out in the fresh air.

People travel by car. Cars take people where they want to go. Sometimes, there are too many cars. Then there is a traffic jam!

Sometimes people take long car trips on the highway. They go to visit relatives or just to see new places.

People travel by train. Trains take people to their jobs in the city. Many trains in the city travel underground. An underground train is called a subway.

Sometimes people travel a long distance by train. They can go all the way across the country. Freight trains take heavy loads of things like food from one place to another.

People travel on the water. Ferry boats carry people and cars short distances. Large ships carry people and freight across the wide ocean.

Sometimes people go in boats just for fun. People sail in sailboats. People row in rowboats. People paddle canoes.

   People travel in the air. When
you need to go a long distance, an
airplane is the fastest way to go.
Jet planes take people to all parts
of the world.

To take a plane, you need to go to an airport. People get to the airport in many different ways. They travel by car, by bus, by van, by taxi, or by subway.

There are so many ways to travel!
What is your favorite way to go?